DATE DUE

1/29/04			
2-1-07			

MARTIN LUTHER KING, JR.

EQUAL RIGHTS LEADERS

Don McLeese

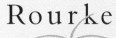

Rourke

Publishing LLC

Vero Beach, Florida 32964

PHOTO CREDITS:
All photos from the Library of Congress

EDITOR: Frank Sloan

COVER DESIGN: Nicola Stratford

Library of Congress Cataloging-in-Publication Data

McLeese, Don.
  Martin Luther King, Jr. / Don McLeese.
     v. cm. — (Equal rights leaders)
Includes bibliographical references (p.   ) and index.
Contents: Civil rights hero — Young M.L. — Bright student — Working
for good — Family man — Civil rights protests — Man of peace — His
dream lives on.
  ISBN 1-58952-286-9
  1. King, Martin Luther, Jr., 1929-1968—Juvenile literature. 2.
African Americans—Biography—Juvenile literature. 3. Civil rights
workers—United States—Biography—Juvenile literature. 4.
Baptists—United States—Clergy—Biography—Juvenile literature. 5.
African Americans—Civil rights—History—20th century—Juvenile
literature. [1. King, Martin Luther, Jr., 1929-1968. 2. Civil rights
workers. 3. Clergy. 4. Civil rights movements—History. 5. African
Americans—Biography.] I. Title.

  E185.97.K5 M385 2002
  323'.092--dc21   2002002044

Printed in the USA

MP/W

TABLE OF CONTENTS

Civil Rights Hero

Martin Luther King, Jr. was the greatest American civil rights hero. During the 1950s and 1960s, King led marches of thousands of people who tried to change society so that it was fair for all Americans. At the time, **African Americans** were often kept from going to the same schools, hotels, or restaurants as white people.

Martin Luther King, Jr. was a great speaker.

Martin Luther King, Jr. fought all his life for rights for African Americans, but not with his fists. As a **Christian** minister, he said it was wrong to hurt even those who were trying to hurt you. Instead of violence, he believed in **non-violence**. He was often joined by his wife, Coretta Scott King.

Martin Luther King, Jr. and Coretta Scott King

Young M.L.

Martin Luther King, Jr., was born in Atlanta, Georgia, on January 15, 1929. His father was a **minister**, the Reverend Martin Luther King, Sr. His mother, Alberta, was a minister's daughter. Because Martin had the same name as his father, everyone called the son "M.L." and his father "Daddy King."

The many faces of Martin Luther King, Jr.

Bright Student

Martin was so smart in school that he skipped both the ninth and twelfth grades. He was only 15 when he started at Morehouse College. He'd once planned to be a doctor, but he decided to become a minister. In 1948, he became associate pastor at Ebenezer Baptist Church in Atlanta. This was the same church where his father and grandfather had been pastors.

Martin speaking at a Philadelphia college

Working For Good

Martin knew it was wrong that society treated African Americans as if they weren't as good as white people. He studied about Mohandas Gandhi, a leader in India who believed in non-violence. Martin learned that you could change society without guns or fighting. When people tried to hurt Martin, he wouldn't hurt them back.

Martin went to jail for his beliefs.

Family Man

When he was getting his doctor's degree at Boston University, Martin met Coretta Scott. He asked her to marry him on their first date! She thought he was joking, but she soon fell in love with him. After they married in 1953, they had four children. Coretta Scott King was a big help to her husband.

Martin with wife, Coretta, and children

Civil Rights Protests

Dr. King was a great speaker and a brave man. His speeches about **civil rights** made thousands of people join him. In 1955, he told followers to quit riding buses in Montgomery, Alabama, until the bus company let African Americans sit where they wanted. Martin was put in jail, and his house was bombed.

Martin and Coretta march in Alabama.

Man of Peace

King led marches and protests in other cities. In 1963, he led the March on Washington, with 250,000 people joining him in the nation's capital. He gave a speech called "I Have a Dream," his dream of freedom for all people. In 1964, he was given the Nobel Peace Prize, one of the world's greatest honors.

Martin at the March on Washington

His Dream Lives On

King was shot to death on April 4, 1968, in Memphis, Tennessee. He was only 39 years old. It was a sad day for the nation to lose such a great man.

In honor of King's birthday, a holiday on the third Monday in January celebrates the life and work of Martin Luther King, Jr.

President Lyndon B. Johnson honors Martin for his civil rights work

Important Dates to Remember

1929   Martin Luther King, Jr., born in Atlanta on
        January 15
1948   King becomes associate pastor at
        Ebenezer Baptist Church in Atlanta
1953   Martin Luther King, Jr., marries
        Coretta Scott
1955   Montgomery bus boycott begins
1963   King leads March on Washington
1964   King given Nobel Peace Prize
1968   King killed on April 4 in Memphis,
        Tennessee

GLOSSARY

African Americans (aff RIH kun uh MARE ih kuns) — black people, Americans whose early relatives came from Africa

Christian (KRISS chun) — a religion that believes in Jesus Christ as the son of God

civil rights (SIV ul RYTS) — the equal rights of every citizen in the country

minister (MIHN iss tur) — pastor or reverend of a church

non-violence (non VY o lence) — refusing to be violent, a peaceful protest

INDEX

Further Reading

Adler, David A. *Dr. Martin Luther King, Jr.* Holiday House, Inc., 2001.
de Kay, James Tertius. *Meet Martin Luther King, Jr.* Random House Books
    for Young Readers, 2001.
Marx, David F. *Martin Luther King, Jr. Day.* Children's Press, 2001.

Websites To Visit

http://www.seattletimes.nwsource.com/mlk

About The Author

Don McLeese is an award-winning journalist whose work has appeared in many
newspapers and magazines. He is a frequent contributor to the World Book Encyclopedia.
He and his wife, Maria, have two daughters and live in West Des Moines, Iowa.